Daddy's girls

Seven lessons in building confidence.
For women and the men who love them.

Monica Grey

GREY SERVICES
a rainbow of solutions

All scripture quotations, unless otherwise indicated, are taken from the New King James Version®. Copyright © 1982 by Thomas Nelson, Inc. Used by permission. All rights reserved.

Scripture quotations marked "Amp." are taken from the Amplified® Bible, Copyright © 1954, 1958, 1962, 1964, 1965, 1987 by The Lockman Foundation Used by permission.
Scripture quotations marked "NIV" are taken from the New International Version®. Copyright © 1973,1978,1984 by International Bible Society. Used by permission. All rights reserved.

British Library Cataloguing in Publication Data

A catalogue record for this book is available from the British Library

Daddy's Girls
ISBN 0-9550555-1-2
Copyright © 2008 by Monica Grey
Published by Grey Services
www.greyservices.com
info@greyservices.com

cover design by Sara Chew

All rights reserved under International Copyright Law. Contents and/or cover may not be reproduced in whole or in part in any form without the express written consent of the Publisher.

The Dedication

To my God, (my true Dad)
Thank you, a million times over for nurturing me and for giving me wisdom, love, patience, guidance, presents, pocket monies, friends, health, life, 2 beautiful and blessed children and 1 handsome and blessed husband.

Dedications

To my mother,

Thank you for teaching me by your example, that women are strong as well as beautiful.

To my grandmother,

Thank you for telling me that I am equal to anyone.

To my daughter,

Thank you for bringing out the girliness in me.

To my sister,

Thank you for teaching me to love.

To my mother-in-law,

Thank you for your pre-marital advice.

To all the women in my life,

Thank you all for being yourselves and showing me in many different shapes, sizes and shades, what confidence is.

Contents

Introduction

Lesson 1 - My testimony

Lesson 2 - God's Blueprint

Lesson 3 - My Blueprint

Lesson 4 - Little women

Lesson 5 - More than role-play

Lesson 6 - Stand Up! (Unless you're Rosa Parks).

Lesson 7 - Daddy's Girls

<u>*Daddy's Girls*</u>

INTRODUCTION

I am not a psychologist, nor am I a doctor. I am a woman; who was once a girl and therefore went through a lot of the hidden pains, fears and feelings of inadequacies that nearly all women have been through. If I ever wrote a book, it would have to be about something that I had conquered, not something I had heard about or was still going through. In March 2004, Daddy pushed a button in me that gave my soul a final clear out of all the low self-esteem junk that was there. The process started many years prior to that though. I am so grateful to my Dad for what He has done in me that I must pass the blessing on. So, here it is, the blessing of wisdom, knowledge and understanding that will build your house on a perfectly solid foundation.

Monica Grey

Lesson 1

My Testimony

They overcame him by the blood of the Lamb and by the word of their testimony.
(Revelation 12 v11)

I was thinking about leaving out this lesson, because I initially thought that it wouldn't sound dramatic enough. However, I have since come to think that dynamism isn't everything and sometimes people want to know that other people go through the niggling little problems that they think only they go through. When I stop to think about it some more, a drastic lack of confidence isn't just a little problem, it used to affect my whole life. At first I needed a reason for my low self-esteem, so I blamed my dad. After all he was never there to compliment me and call me 'his little princess'. Then God reminded me that He was with me from before I was born and was and still is my ever-present Dad. Then I needed a pity party. I constantly blamed everyone else for everything bad that happened to me, so that they would see how hard-done-by I was and feel sorry for me. They did feel sorry. And then what? It didn't change how I felt inside. I used to spend every Christmas and New Year's Eve alone crying. To this day, I am still not sure why I did that. Perhaps it had something to do with not ever getting all of the things that everyone else had that would make me 'happier'. I was uncomfortable interacting with the opposite sex, probably because I had grown up in a predominantly female family. But God gave me genuine male friends, one in particular who was naturally affectionate and greeted everyone with hugs. At first I was uncomfortable, but I soon began to see God's purpose in the people that He put around me. To put it bluntly I felt rotten about myself and that rottenness oozed into everything that I thought, said and did. One Valentine's day, I looked into the mirror and burst into tears. I was thoroughly depressed. I had never, and felt that I would never get a Valentine's card. Why? It just wasn't fair? Would nobody ever love me enough to buy and send me a Valentine's card? Just as I was about to make myself really sick with useless decadence, the Lord whispered into my heart. 'The True Vine is your Valentine'. Talk about meeting me where I was. Instead of telling me not to be so stupid and who cares about ridiculously soppy pink cards anyway, He came to me and started a process in me that changed my life forever. Yes, I was a Christian. I had been baptised and all, but that old me kept on trying to be resurrected. It kept on telling me that I couldn't be who God said I was, or that I would never be married and that nobody would ever like me for who I was. I used to fantasise about a rich long-lost aunt or uncle who would come to get me one day. They never came. Someone unspeakably better did. The Lord gradually gave me confidence-building lessons. He told me to look in the mirror and say 'I love me' out loud. I shared a bedroom with my sister at the time, so I had to pick my moments! After a while though I didn't feel so ridiculous saying it and I actually started believing what I was saying. God started to show me my internal value, that was based upon Who I belonged to and what He had for me to do in this life. So I found purpose in my talents and the things that I enjoyed doing. He taught me how to manage money, but I learned that one the hard way, by getting into unnecessary debts. He told me that

I FOUND PURPOSE IN MY TALENTS AND THE THINGS THAT I ENJOYED DOING

it was alright to buy clothes for myself every now and again, which I never did, I seemed to think that I wasn't worth the bother. By the time that the Lord had finished with me I was actually able to honestly say that I liked myself. During the early part of 2004, the Lord did one final spring clean in my soul. He pushed a button and I immediately felt different. I said to my husband Paul, "P, I feel different." He looked at me as if to say a slow "okaaay." But a few days later, after he heard the way I spoke about my plans, my purpose, and myself he said to me, "Mon, you're different." And that, if you like, is my testimony. It is what I used to be and what I am now, different, unique, everything that my Dad says that I am. Most of all, I am happy with me, even when I have a not-so-good hair day, or I feel like wearing my very baggy jumper, (around the house mind you), I still feel priceless. Why? Because my confidence which was misplaced for years, has been replaced right smack bang in the centre of God. I have come to the realisation that I do not have to *feel* confident all of time, in every area of my life, in order to *be* confident.

Daughters generally attribute their high level of confidence to their father's input in their lives. I can testify to that. My Dad has always called me His darling and His precious. He has always provided for me, but unlike some father's He didn't spoil me by giving me every one of my whimsical requests. He taught me discipline but He also pulled strings for me in high places. He has been a great Dad and He still is. Right now, I am enjoying my relationship with Him more than ever. I am also enjoying my daughter's relationship with my husband, her dad. It serves as an earthly example of how precious my Dad has been to me and still is. More than anything, I want my children and the children who I come into contact with, to *know* their Dad as well and to appreciate Him as their Dad. More than anything I want you to experience the confident rest that comes from really *knowing* Him. Because when it is all said and done, that is what He wants too.

Homework

TASK ONE

Make or send yourself a Valentine's Day card. Make sure that you use the words 'I love me' in it.

Lesson 2

The Blueprint

For I know the thoughts and plans that I have for you, says the Lord, thoughts and plans for welfare and peace and not for evil, to give you hope in your final outcome.
(Amp. Jeremiah 29 v11)

Before we discuss your womanhood, let me first inform you that you are really a man! Shocked? I thought you would be. Let us get it straight though, you are *man* not *male*. And ' man' in the sense of human kind. God said in Genesis, 'Let Us make man in Our image'. What exactly did He mean by that? Well, when you look into the mirror what do you see? Your reflection of course, or your *image*. When God the Father, discussed with The Son and The Holy Spirit, how we were to be made, there was a unanimous decision, we had to be made just like God, reflecting everything that He is. For those of you who have children, you should be able to understand this concept. Your cute little bundle has barely come to terms with being propelled into this big, noisy world and everyone who sees her is telling you that she looks like mummy or daddy, or her grandma Couscous or aunty Semolina. Then your little bundle becomes a bigger bundle and starts crawling around then walking then talking, and you can soon see for yourself that your child is a very good reflection of you. She says what you say in the tone that you say it, (with her hands on hips and all)! She even does the things that you do. The children that we give birth to, very often reflect our image. This is true partly because our kids are in our presence a lot, so we rub off on them. In the same way we are to reflect God's image when we are 'born again' of the spirit and spend time in His presence, to let Him rub off on us. I say that to say this. Whoever God is, we essentially are, because God made us in His image, like Him. But the Bible says that He made 'man' in His image. Well that is just my point. I believe that there is man in all of us, male or female. I am very glad that God made me a woman, but I am even more glad that He called me 'man' first. Man is who God made in His image, so when I think of manhood, I think of stability, faithfulness, integrity, provision, solutions, fun and leadership. Now, I realise that for many of you, the word 'manhood' brings up very, let us say, different concepts. That's alright, (for now), you have just started reading this book. By the time you have read to the end, you should have lost your hang-ups. God knew that in order for us to subdue the earth and have dominion, we would need cooperation between men and women. Women have and still do contribute excellence to the smooth running of this world. And for those of you who keep tripping up on what mother Eve did wrong, let me help you to forgive her with my definition of confidence. *Confidence is, knowing Whose you are even though the whole world is pointing the finger of blame at you.* Good marriages inevitably share their goodness with their churches, businesses, communities, and the world. *But* the foundation of this male/female unity is manhood. If I can accept that God called me 'man', then I will understand that my entire person is founded on stability, faithfulness, integrity, provision, solutions, fun and leadership. If I keep this in the forefront of my mind, I won't crash miserably when my femininity blossoms. I'm sure that you will agree that our femininity has a not-so-cute way of emerging at a particular time of the month. There are some days when we feel like staying in bed all day, or eating chocolate all day or shopping, or just crying for nothing in particular. Then at another time, we are mentally as sharp as a knife and physically able to do much more than we may normally do. During these emotional roller-coaster rides, I try to remember that I have a spirit-man, a part of me that is tuned into God and is like God. This helps me to better subdue the earth, (as it is local to me), and have dominion. Emotional fragility and unpredictability will subdue nothing. God's original plan is for us to prosper and for that to happen, we need to first accept that God gave us a spirit and train ourselves to be led by our spirit-man and not our female body or soul. No I don't mean that we should never eat chocolate or have late lie-ins or pamper ourselves, (I'm hoping that there will be strawberry cheesecake in heaven!) But we have to remember that how we behave towards others affects them for better or worse. Being rude, snappy and impatient, and then blaming it on our hormones, will just not cut it on the day of reckoning. God's grace is always sufficient for us to overcome negative emotions and our loved ones may not understand forever. God plans to prosper you in every area of your life, so if it is less than what God gives you, do not accept it. If necessary, and possible, hide yourself away, pray and cry it out, but come back remembering who you are. That is, created in God's image, created to have dominion and to rule over a unique sphere, perfectly and wonderfully made, a child of The King of kings, need I go on?

The most fail-proof method of getting and maintaining a healthy self-esteem is to anchor your confidence in the One Who has perfect confidence. Our Dad wants more than anything to have a close relationship with us. Contrary to the portrayals of 'Christianity' that have kept a lot of people away from Him, He is all about love, in fact He is Love. For some of you the mention of the word dad immediately resurfaces emotional pains. I understand. But one thing that I have learned is that my Dad is perfect. He really is. He only has excellence planned for us, but the thing is, that excellence is only going to be found in Him. If you can't yet say that you know Him and love Him, then I ask you to get to know Him. Find a Bible and ask Him to guide your reading. You'll be surprised at how awesome getting to know Him will be. It will affect your daily activities, as well as your soul. And He will begin to roll out the plans that He has for you; plans to prosper you and to give you a future. In fact, you will eventually find out that He has been working on you since the day you were born, and that nothing you have gone through or are going through will be wasted. You'll see.

HOMEWORK

TASK TWO
- Buy a Bible or
- Read the Bible and
- Get to know Him.

Lesson 3
My Blueprint

Write the vision...
(Habakkuk 2 v2)

May I suggest that women are instinctively leaders? Our ability to balance many different activities at one time, and to perform them well is testament to us having both man-ness and woman-ness in us. The world sees it in how we bear and nurture our children and grandchildren, with or without help. They see it in how we support our men and lead corporations; at the same time. They see it in how we outlive stress, hardship and physical wear and tear, despite the odds. Women who know what they want in life and business, and go for it with everything, tend to be labelled as aggressive. The passion that exudes when you live your life to its maximum purpose should never be called aggression, permit it only to be called what it is. Confidence. If you agree with me, then may we proceed to look at ourselves using the concept of a business plan?

Executive Summary

All good businesses solve a problem. They offer something that people need and are willing to pay for. If you were to see yourself as a business or a company, what unique purpose do you exist for? What is it that you can do, in the way that you do it, that no one else can? That very thing could be your life's purpose, and the sooner you are able to define your purpose in a simple statement, the better. As a teenager, I knew that my purpose was to teach children. As I have progressed in life, so too has the definition of my purpose. I now state that my purpose is 'to educate young minds.' This has become my life mission statement and it keeps me focussed. It is the sieve through which all of my activities go. If it is in line with my purpose, then I go for it with all of my heart. If it is not, then I do not go for it at all; it is as simple as that. As I write, I am fulfilling my purpose by educating all of you who read my books. I am a full-time home-working mother and wife, so by nurturing and educating my two children is another way that I am fulfilling my purpose. There are many ways in which we can fulfil our life purpose and that is what keeps our lives exciting.

It is important for me to state that my purpose is in line with my husband's purpose. My husband's mission statement is 'To inspire, encourage and educate,' and as you can see, mine fits very neatly into his. So as I pursue my life's purpose, I am also fulfilling the family vision. As a married woman, I could never pursue a vision that is completely different from my husband's. It is true that I am a unique and different person to my husband, but Dad is looking, not so much at what I achieve, but how I achieve it, and my willingness to agree with my husband and submit to his leadership should be manifested in what I choose to do with my life. Dad is pleased with unity and He says that a house divided will never stand.

What is your life's purpose? Can you define it in a simple statement? How are you or how will you fulfil your purpose? Because of your purpose, what one over-arching thing must you do, before you die?

I would like to call that thing, your life's aim. Mine is to develop a thriving international network of schools and as you can see, it is linked directly to my life purpose. When you have an aim, you are better able to fulfil your purpose, because you can then decide what steps you need to take in order to reach your aim. The word 'steps' is a verb, an action word; so what small things should you do in order to achieve your aim?

OPERATIONAL PLAN

Here is an example of my operational plan. Feel free to use the same format to map out yours.

Life Purpose: To Educate Young Minds

Life Aim: To develop a thriving international network of schools.

Life Goals:

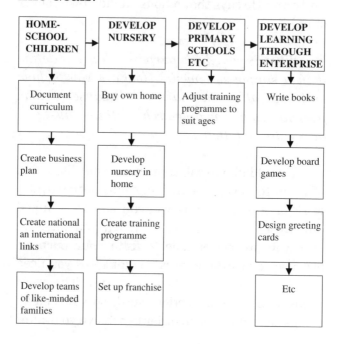

Time plan

Age \ Activity	30-35 Years	36-40 Years	41-45 Years	46-50 Years	51-? Years
Develop nursery	■				
Develop curriculum	■	■			
Develop primary, secondary etc. schools	■	■	■	■	■

I do not mean to force you to use the format that I have provided; the most important thing is that you have a plan. If you do not plan your life, then you simply plan to fail. Now you can make your operational plan as detailed as you would like to, but keep in mind that it is essentially a life plan, so do not be disheartened at the enormity of it all and do remember that it should be perceived as a working document and something that can be added to and edited as your life unfolds.

FINANCES

There is nothing so damaging to self-esteem as being poor. Having no money and being forced to depend upon others for financial support is a situation that can leave us feeling trapped and without options. Let us get one thing clear; we always have options. And when it comes to finances, we need to weigh up our options very carefully. Before addressing the subject of getting more money, let me ask you a question? How do you think about money? Sadly, a lot of women do not feel responsible for thinking about money, but the attitude you have towards it determines the direction that money moves in relation to you, towards you or away from you. First of all, what does Daddy think about money? You who are well versed in all things biblical, will probably be chanting, 'the love of money is the root of all evil', 1st Timothy 6 verse 10; but what about 'money answereth all things', Ecclesiastes 10 verse 19? Isn't it just like us to emphasise the one negative description of money in the Bible and forget all the other positive ones. The Vines Concise Dictionary of Bible Words offers a definition of money that I would like to focus on. *Chrema* (Greek), which means 'a thing one uses.' Just like our clothes, food, pens, bags, computers etc, money is to be used and used wisely. From my experiences with Dad and what He has taught me about money, I would like to suggest that He is not so concerned about giving you more money, as He is about getting you to use what you already have wisely.

After reading and studying Proverbs 4, the following principles came to mind: wisdom, instruction, understanding, your mind, God's Word, direction, focus, discipline, dominion, rule, lord. In order to change my attitude towards money, God had to consistently shape me according to these principles. I have done an accounting course and applied what I learned to my household finances, because Dad expects us to be good stewards of what He has given us. Our top-most priority when it comes to our money is to tithe, i.e. to give the first 10% of our income to God. When I started tithing to God, by giving my first 10% to my local church, He started to influence my attitude towards money and when He knew that I was absolutely capable of handling more money wisely, He gave me more; sometimes through miraculous means, but most of the time through pretty 'normal' means. Dad does not waste anything, so He will not pour monetary blessings into a life that will waste it.

How do you prioritise your money? What financial systems do you have in place for receiving and investing your money?

Here are some suggestions:

I. Open different accounts for different things, e.g. tithes account, car account, food account, clothes account, holiday

account, birthdays account etc. Budget accordingly, and when you need to pay for petrol, only use money from the car account.
II. If you are able to pay bills online, do so. It saves so much time, time that can be used to get more money.
III. Don't think of your main income as your only possible source of income. Include gifts, benefits, bank interest and use your creativity. And don't tell me that you're not creative; God is so you are too! You could earn money aside from your main income by thinking. Someone said that money comes when you solve someone's problem. Think in the realm of your purpose and your gift will make way for you. Ask Dad to give you witty ideas, but make sure that when He gives them to you, that you work on them. It takes something to happen for something to happen!
IV. How can you cut down on bills/other monies spent, even in small ways? Could you make your own lunch? And/or your own clothes? Could you change your phone tariff or speak for a little less time on the phone? Do you

'CONFIDENCE' IS ALLOWING YOU TO BE SATISFIED WITH YOU

throw away and buy anew unnecessarily? Stop looking at what others have and focus on your purpose. 'Confidence' is allowing you to be satisfied with you.

MARKETING

In business terms, marketing refers, in part, to how we advertise our products or services to the people that we want to attract. Whether we intend to or not, we make an impression, positive or negative, on the people who we come into contact with. If I know where I am going, then I will dress the part. If you were invited to a wedding and turned up in jogging bottoms and a scruffy t-shirt, I am pretty sure that you would receive peculiar stares, and rightly so. If someone has thought enough of you to invite you to their special occasion, then the least you owe them is to do your best to look the part, (that is of course assuming that jogging bottoms and a t-shirt isn't your best, but even if it was you could still manage a neat t-shirt). I won't write at length about clothing, because I realise that women in different countries, lifestyles and roles will wear vastly different kinds of clothes. I will just state the obvious, that people, wrongly or rightly, make pre-judgements about us according to how we dress. My advice is 'dress to purpose'. Go back to your life mission statement and imagine yourself achieving it. What do *you* think *you* should look like? My emphasis is on what suits you, over what the magazines and advertisements say you should wear. You don't have to have a huge clothing allowance to be able to dress to purpose, you just need to have the wisdom for it. God gives the wisdom; we just have to use it. How will you know when you have got it right? All you need to do is set your own measurements, do not depend on other people telling you that you look good, although that should and may happen. Find a full-length mirror and perform your normal movements. Are parts of your body being shown, that will give a wrong impression? Will you sweat through the fabric? Will your baby or toddler over-crease or soil the outfit? Do you feel 100% comfortable? If you have met your own targets, then compliment yourself and walk through your front door.

It is not merely with our clothing that we attract or repel people. Our facial expressions, posture and the words we use in the way that we use them all speak volumes about our confidence levels and who we are. How we market ourselves to the people that we meet is central to how they treat us.

Much could be said about facial expressions and tone of voice, but I think it would be more beneficial for you to concentrate on fixing your attitudes, and then the external will automatically be pleasant. This is not true of course when it comes to physical exercise. Thinking about exercising is not the same as doing it, and doing it has so much benefit, that you should make time for it. It obviously makes you fitter; it releases pleasant hormones; it makes you more disciplined; it gives you more energy; it makes you sweat (or should I say glow), which is good for your skin; and it really does make you feel good about yourself, which is essential to improving your confidence.

I used to have such a stern looking face and I fooled myself into thinking that it wasn't really an accurate depiction of what was on the inside of me. The only way that I have proven to work when it comes to changing my aura is to spend quality time in, (no, not necessarily the beauty salon, hairdressers, health spa, clothing boutique, gym or nail shop; although I highly recommend the health spa); it's in God's presence. I find that whenever I have invested real time and energy in praising God in spirit and in truth, not only do I feel more peaceful within me, but I also get those longing looks from my husband that you wives know about ... God has a way of making you attractive. I do not want to confuse attractiveness with beauty; God gave us all beauty, individually and collectively in our diversity.

I am referring to something quite different, something that draws another person to you and gives you favour. It can sometimes make you completely irresistible to others, but as with everything that God gives to us, we must remember who gets the credit for it. Don't attribute this type of magnetism to your own efforts, otherwise you will be bordering pride; and pride is ugly. Having confidence makes you humble.

HAVING CONFIDENCE MAKES YOU HUMBLE

The Team

The people you have around you will either lift you higher or tear you down. There are no neutralisers in your life. As a leader, you need to decide who you are going to allow the privilege of sowing seeds into your mind. Just as employers actively seek people to work for them, you need to actively seek people to work with. Here is a simple checklist that I have found to be very useful when seeking out the right people:

1. Pray. Ask Daddy to guide you in finding friends, associates, mentors etc. Ask Him to give you wisdom in choosing who you should

or should not open up to. Then follow the guidance that comes from His peace.
2. Observe potential friends etc from a close distance before jumping into friendships. Will they enhance your purpose?
3. Consider how they bring up their children. Like it or not, your children will probably become friends with children of your friends.
4. Departmentalise yourself. Someone may be a good friend, but not necessarily a good financial advisor. You should be able to tell the difference.
5. Research the person on the Internet. Don't make up your mind totally, but if they have written a book or been involved in the wider community or politics etc, you will have an idea of the kind of person you are approaching.
6. Concentrate on being a good friend yourself. She who has friends must first show herself friendly.
7. Understand that not all friendships are lifelong. Some people are in your life for a short but significant moment.

OPPORTUNITIES

Someone said that you shouldn't ask God for opportunities but you should ask Him to make you ready when opportunities come. If you look at your life carefully, you will see a plethora of opportunities waiting to be taken advantage of. That person's phone number tucked away in your purse could be the opportunity to launch your greeting card business. That neighbour, who plays his music too loud, could be the catalyst for you to move to a different area. The crazy looking guy at church, who wears sports socks with his suits, could be your future husband!! Think about it.

COMPETITION

Do you view every other woman as a target to be aimed at or a friend to be known? I used to constantly compare myself to all other women. I noted whether they had better clothes than I did, a better voice, a better posture. And somewhere along the way I would end up copying what I saw. I have since realised that I have my own niche. No one else can be me, so I stick to my own tastes even though I may admire and compliment my sisters'. Did you know that take-away restaurants deliberately open up next to each other to benefit from the crowds that will come just because there is more choice? Not to mention high street shops are often clustered under one or two major names, so while you think you are getting a better deal by going next door to Susu's Toiletries, the owner couldn't care less which one you went to, he still gets your money. Let's have a similar mindset about our sisterhood. Realise that it doesn't really matter who wins this time, because if you win, I win and vice versa.

Resources

You know that old question 'if you were stuck on a desert island, what 3 objects would you want the most?' Well answer it for your life. Which three things do you prioritise as the most important objects in fulfilling your life's purpose? My answer: My Bible, my pen and my notepad.

Risks

If you do not allow yourself to fail by taking risks, then you will never really prove that you love yourself. Risk-takers are confident people. Of course you should manage the risks as well as you can, but after all the assessment and research, go for it. As daughters of God, we really should be more willing to take risks, because although we shouldn't go to Dad to find out what this week's lottery numbers

Risk-takers are confident people

are, He is all for guiding us and whispering into our spirits the right thing to do or not do. But then of course, if you don't get the expected result, accept it as a lesson learned and move on.

Homework

TASK THREE
Create your life business plan.

Lesson 4
Little Women

Older women should train younger women.

Every woman is a daughter; we were all brought up by someone. Some of us are sisters, some are wives and some are mothers, grandmothers, great-grandmothers, great great grandmothers etc. I would like us to explore some of these fascinating roles together, because the roles that we play, and how well we play them often feed into how we feel about ourselves.

The first of the roles that I would like to consider is that of daughter or granddaughter. My advice to you girlies is simple. LEARN FAST, WORK HARD and KEEP SWEET. This is what I used to keep me on the straight and narrow, and it has helped me to hold my head high in confidence to this day.

LEARN FAST

The moment you were born, you started learning and you haven't stopped. While you were a baby you did not have much control over what you learned, but as you grow older, you can decide what books to read, what music to listen to and who to have as friends. Books are a very good way to spend your time and any money that you might have. Remember that girl at school that always has her face in a book, well now it's time to take a leaf out of her book, so to speak. She has the right idea. Not only will it help you with your schoolwork, it will also mean that you grow to love reading for the enjoyment of it, not just because you have to. Not to mention it just might help to keep you out of trouble! When I was a young girl, I absolutely loved reading and my mum and grandma encouraged me to read by making sure that I had loads of books to choose from. I especially loved reading novels by female authors like Charlotte Bronte; I even got into the Virginia Andrews series, (way too old for me, but they didn't do any lasting harm). I read encyclopaedias; short stories, poems and I did my best to read a part of the Bible everyday. The best thing about Bible-reading is that you actually get to live what you learn. For example, you may be going through a really rough time in your life and you read in the Bible that God comforts you so that you can comfort others. Straight away you can see that if you focus on helping other people with their problems, your own problems tend not to seem half as bad, or at least it takes your mind off it for a while. As a rule, whatever you put into yourself is what you will get out. Books about other people's lives are a good place to start; these are called biographies or autobiographies. There are some that have been written for young people, look in the library, bookshops or the Internet. Biographies are a good place to find out how other people did things and why. By reading them, you will learn from other people's mistakes and you won't have to make the same mistakes yourself.

Just like reading, listening to music is a brilliant way to learn. I won't go into this too much, but do not be tempted to just follow the crowd and listen to what everyone your age listens to. Look at it as research and find out about other types of music. Classical, jazz, Gospel are types that I would recommend and there are so many variations to Gospel music, Gospel reggae, Gospel rock, Gospel country and western. Listen around and find something that suits your personality and most importantly has wholesome lyrics.

FRIENDS. Don't you just love 'em? Don't they also have a way of getting on your nerves every now and again? There is a saying that goes, 'you can't choose your siblings, but you can choose your friends, so choose wisely.' This is a lot easier said than done. A lot of friendships are actually made for us. By groups teachers put us in at school, children of our parents' friends. You really only have the choice of whether or not to stay friends with some of these people. Whatever your decision, it might help to know that you probably won't stay close friends with most of the people you hang around with now. You will go to different secondary schools; colleges, universities and you will almost certainly have different jobs or lines of business. When Jesus was on this earth He had loads of people who He hung around with, I'm talking hundreds, but out of over 100 people who followed Him around, only 12 are well-known by us, only 3 were very close to Him and out of those 3, there was only 1 who He considered His very best friend.

When you find that you do have the ability to choose your friends here is some handy advice:

1. Never jump straight into a friendship with the first person that shows an interest in you. Take some time to stand back and see if she is the type of person you want to be around.
2. Strike up a conversation. If she gossips about other people, she will gossip about you. If she talks about herself most of the time and doesn't ask about you, you probably won't be able to share your problems

with her. If you find yourself finishing off each other's sentences, you've probably found a soul mate. And if you can make each other laugh, take her phone number.
3. Ask yourself the question, do you like her? And I don't mean the clothes she wears or her hairstyles or her gadgets. Is she a nice person? Because like it or not, you will start to act a little bit like whoever you spend time with. Show me your company and I will tell you who you are.
4. Lastly, do not just look for friends who are the same age as you are. Older people will be able to teach you a lot about life, but make sure they are not total strangers. Make older female friends who know your family, maybe someone from your church or other group. Don't think that old equals boring, trust me, some of my funniest friends are elderly people with a sense of humour and a half. They also give you a snippet of your history, you'll know what things your mother really got up to when she was your age:)

WORK HARD

My next piece of advice might make me sound a bit like your mother. I am going to have the high expectation that you are already working hard with your schoolwork. I am sure that I do not need to stress the point that you get one real chance at school and you don't want to waste time doing re-sits. But your education is not the only thing that you should work hard at. At home, you may see your mother doing a lot, as mothers do. Don't just watch, join in. Not only will your mother greatly appreciate the help (believe me, she will). You will benefit from it too. I know you don't believe me, but there is a skill in housework, especially cooking that you will pick up from your mum and it will make life that much easier for you when you leave home. If your mum is like my mum was and doesn't like cooking, then learn everything else from her; (cleaning, laundering, gardening, child-rearing, knitting, having fun), and go to that older friend that you made, to learn the cooking. If or when you get married, these skills will be as precious to you as the sparkling diamond ring on your finger.

You will also benefit from working hard in your local community. You know, the local church is having a summer fete and wants volunteers. The local Age Concern needs people to befriend their elderly. The local hospital needs volunteers to clear out their gardens. Or the local dog's home needs walkers. There's just so much to choose from and if you do end up being one of those choice ladies who remain unmarried until you are thirty-something, you will be so busy that you won't even notice!

KEEP SWEET

Now, here is where I get very serious with you all. There is a trend nowadays for young ladies to have sex or get really intimate with just about anybody. It's not on. Let me tell you officially that it is not trendy, nor is it sensible. Let me assume that you will be married one day, with that in mind, WAIT! Do you realise how precious your virginity is to you and to God your Father. It is a gift from you to your husband; so don't give it away to anyone else. Now I realise that I may be speaking to some of you who have already given it away and to some others who have had it stolen from you. Firstly to those who have given it away. Stop. Now. Don't allow yourself to continue just because you think that you have already messed up. God is able to work with someone who's heart is in the right place, much more than someone else who may be a virgin physically, but their mind is all messed up.

Now to you who have suffered abuse. Whether it was recent or distant, I want you to know that it doesn't take away anything from who you are. Because you didn't give it, you still have it, and don't you forget it. Our Heavenly Dad is more interested in our hearts than our bodies, so although He will heal your body, He also told me to tell you that He loves you and that what has happened to you, is not who you are. You are His daughter and He did not allow it to happen, but He will turn around what has happened and take away the pain. One day despite it all, you will be able to smile and even laugh out loud, because through His miraculous restorative power, He will give you your sweetness back!

Homework

TASK FOUR
Help your daughter (and your son, god-child etc), to make their life business plan.

Lesson 5
More Than Role-play

A capable, intelligent, and virtuous woman – who is he who can find her?
(Amp. Proverbs 31 v10)

SISTERHOOD

I have the mixed blessing of having both brothers and sisters. Not to mention loads of cousins who are like sisters to me. Being the eldest of four was made slightly easier because the cousins that I was closest to were all older than me. One of my cousins epitomises the perfect older sister in one very important matter. Dress sense. She had so many clothes that her wardrobe door often couldn't be closed and even more importantly most of them could fit me. My advice to sisters is to share and share alike. Not just clothes. Share your toys, secrets, money, friends, traumas, (please don't share your boyfriends)! Life is better when it is shared. Do each other's hair, paint each other's finger nails and toe nails. Do facials, do dancing, do kickboxing if you like, do anything wholesome, just make the most of the fact that your parents have given you a ready-made companion. Like her or not, you're stuck with her, so make the most of the relationship. On the other hand, having a brother especially a younger one can be a bit of a pain in the neck. Boys are just not the same as girls, but they have their good points. Those of you who have older brothers should already know what it is to be protected from bullies, (unless of course, your older brother is the bully). It may also help to think of brothers as well as sisters, as though they are work colleagues. Think about it, your daily housework duties are your job and your siblings are fellow employees. No prizes for guessing who your boss is, (no, it's not dad)! Anyway, having brothers and sisters will prepare you brilliantly for the world of work. You will have the same lazy workmate who lets you do all the work. The same work bully who harasses you behind the boss's back and the one who pulls out a sick note on spring-cleaning day. I am at a stage in my life where my siblings don't really affect my everyday life anymore. I have a nostalgic thought or two where my siblings and cousins are concerned, but what I really love is our family gatherings, where there really is no end to the laughter, conversation and enjoyment of seeing us all mixed up with babies, toddlers, in-laws and the smell of fried chicken.

WIFEHOOD

You have now left home and someone has found you. Not just anyone, the man of your dreams. And he has made you his wife. There are 5 distinct stages of wifehood: the newlywed, the first child, subsequent children, the made it wife and 'us' again.

The Newlywed

The newlywed has it pretty easy. Just herself and her husband to please. Yet most of us make the obvious mistake of trying so hard to be the perfect wife that we pretend to be who we are not. I have a friend who admitted to making this mistake by diligently ironing all of her husband's clothes before putting them away, including his very long jeans. She said that she used to struggle because she is so short, and couldn't hold his jeans up without them touching the floor. She soon stopped that when she realised that she couldn't keep it up. Some women iron the clothes as soon as they are dry, others iron to wear. Not only is there logic in both methods it really is a simple case of preference. If however, you succumb to the misconceived notion that every wife must have dinner on the table by 5pm daily, must keep the house spotlessly clean 24 hours a day and never have a hair protruding from your legs or your armpits, you are setting yourself up for failure at some point or another. If you don't believe me then fast forward to the section on having your first child! Now of course, if you have the luxury of having a chef, a cleaner and a personal hairstylist, manicurist etc, oh yes and someone promising 24 hour childcare, then this won't apply to you, so you should fast forward to the 'first child' section. If however, like the majority of us you do most of the housekeeping yourself, then please take my advice and start as you mean to go on. Please do not get me wrong; you should aim to do all of these things, prepare meals, (unless your hubby likes doing it and is a better cook than you are), tidy the house and look after yourself, but just bear in mind that the standard you set now, will be what your husband will come to expect. If you know that you really don't believe in keeping the furniture dust-free, but prefer to keep layers of dust for finger-writing purposes, then tell him from the outset, (preferably before he marries you to give him a chance to opt out)! It's only fair and if he really understands what love is, he will marry you anyway because the love criteria are patience and kindness, not 'can she clean and can she cook?'

The First Child

Then comes the moment of ecstasy, (literally), when you become a mother. What more can

I say? For those of you who are mothers, you already know everything there is to know about joy and laughter, pain and tears, sacrifice and giving up everything that used to mean something to you. I will though share something that I am slowly learning to do. We need to release our children. Not to strangers necessarily or people who have seriously different values to ourselves or to dangerous situations; but that goes without saying. We need to teach them how to live, in varying degrees, without us. This is one of the hardest aspects of motherhood, after all, who can honestly say that they enjoy being surplus to requirements? It is however, necessary. They will leave sooner or later anyway, so break into it gently. From which point should you start teaching them independence? From birth. And no, I do not mean that you should allow your newborn baby to discover the perils of fixing her own bottle or giving themselves a bath, but believe it or not, there are things that even a newborn can start to comprehend. Notice. Your baby cries, you pick him up and feed him they learn to cry if they are hungry. Now what if your baby is quietly awake in his cot. Most first-timers will pick baby up and start an entertainment session, thereby, not allowing baby to learn that it is ok to spend time alone entertaining oneself. And what of your toddler or pre-schooler? The tendency is to tell them the answers to all of life's enigmas. For example, 'don't rock on your chair, or you will fall off'; 'don't eat all of those chocolates or you will feel sick'; or better still 'don't play with matches or you'll burn the house down.' I am not for a moment suggesting that you should allow your children to do any of these things, but just think of how many of these instructions we feed into their inquisitive minds, consequently, not allowing them to find out for themselves the consequences of their actions. If we really stopped to think about it, a lot of what we say isn't wholly accurate. How many times have you rocked on a chair, without falling off it? Or eaten too many choccies without feeling sick? And matches with no striking bit, could be the source of endless hours of harmless fun.

Your children need to know that there are other people in the world who love them and would take care of them. Especially useful if you have just threatened to throw them out of the house if they talk to you like that again! If you are anything like me and feel that no one can look after your children just like you can. You're right! But that is the point. Other people will give your children different experiences and life lessons that they would otherwise miss out on. For instance, I am not particularly fond on any member of the animal kingdom. So if it were down to me, Jerry and Jahdai would not come into any sort of contact with animals. And even if I allowed them to have a goldfish or two, I certainly wouldn't be able to show them how to take them out of the tank for cleaning! (I mean I really wouldn't)! So I depend upon my husband's love of nature and animals to develop my offspring into well-rounded individuals. But seeing that if Paul had a pet, I would have to have one too, (so he doesn't), I allow Jerry to enjoy the company of my mother's budgies or my uncle's dog or brother-in-law's kittens. He therefore will not inherit my unfortunate dislike of animals. This is already evident in his tendency to proudly bring worms (that belong in the garden), into the living room, (that should be worm-free)! Learning to release our children will enable us to secure close friends and family as rather reliable babysitters!

Subsequent Children

You may think that having one child is very similar to having two. Think again! When you have more than one child, you are constantly thinking in twos, or threes etc. The first several months of a new baby in the family can feel like a tornado has hit your home, literally leaving the house undone, dinners undone, your body and soul undone, and the siblings undone, (especially a firstborn experiencing sibling-dom for the first time), and if your husband felt left out when your first child was born, he may feel completely put out now. I began to prepare Jerry for brotherhood a long time before Jahdai was even conceived. I bought him books and videos showing positive brotherly relationships and highlighted sibling relationships amongst his friends. By the time Jahdai got here, he was pretty well prepared for the 'baby to come out of the tummy'. During my pregnancy, Jerry often got impatient with his forthcoming sister and tried to deliver her before time, but nothing was quite like actually seeing this baby out in the open. I had home births with both of my children, so Jerry came home from nanny's house about six hours after Jahdai was born. His expression could not have been more telling. He was eventually able to voice his emotions with this single instruction, "ok mummy, you can put the baby back in the tummy now." For all of my preparation he was still uneasy. Bless him, he was a darling for the first few months, but then he started to mimic the baby and misbehave for the attention that used to be all his. I could often see him reminiscing about a time when he was the only one. I had to keep telling myself over and over again, this is not my fault, all firstborns go through similar experiences. It was so hard seeing my first born in such turmoil.

He loved Jahdai right from the beginning, but when he was told off for spewing his food out of his mouth and Jahdai was not, he just could not handle the injustice of it, even though I tried to explain. Do not allow your confidence to be shattered because of temporary experiences. In other words, it will pass. There comes a time, maybe when your newest arrival starts to crawl or walk, that your children will actually start ganging up together against you; what a delightful thought!

DO NOT ALLOW YOUR CONFIDENCE TO BE SHATTERED BECAUSE OF TEMPORARY EXPERIENCES

My husband has the patience of Job. During Jahdai's baby stages, he often had to put up with me worrying about her lack of appetite, or her dry skin or petite frame, each time he would try to tell me not to worry but I wouldn't have any of it. Although I knew that worrying was going to do no good whatsoever, I somehow felt as though by stating what was wrong, I was showing myself the expert, the one who knew everything about our children. Now what I am admitting here is not easy for me to do, but it is necessary. You see, us mothers tend to want to believe that our husbands do not notice that our children have another need after playing. Hard as it may be to believe, dads want to be a parent as well. The best way to give yourself more time and allow your children to experience their dad's parenting is leave him to it. Stop telling him what to do, how to do it and when to do it. He will work it out, just like you did. Not to mention your moaning will make him feel like a spare tyre and that won't be any good for your marriage. As well as all of that, make some daily, weekly and monthly time for just the two of you. Even if that means getting dressed up to have a romantic dinner-date at home, just make sure that someone else cooks the dinner! By nurturing your marriage, you will automatically act like a wife and in turn you will feel like a woman and will hopefully remember to treat yourself like one.

When experiencing my time of nursing a young baby and nurturing a pre-schooler, I found it really easy to feel sorry for myself a lot and wonder what I had done wrong. However, whenever I went to Daddy about it, He always told me to get on with it. After all, I was wasting precious time by just sitting down asking the same useless question over and over again. 'How can I find more time?' I finally came to the conclusion that I wasn't ever going to find more time, but I could start using the time that I did have more wisely. My Dad gave me a strategy that worked for me. At first I gave myself the target of just 5 minutes a day. If I could just use 5 minutes in a 24-hour cycle, to do some writing or something else pertaining to my life vision, over a short space of time I would achieve a lot. It worked. Because I was easy on myself, by just asking for 5 minutes a day, I did not feel pressured because I knew that even if I couldn't manage to find the time during the day, after the kids were in bed, I could afford at least 5 minutes then. My Dad was teaching me the effectiveness of consistency. The next thing He wanted to teach me was the necessity of sacrifice. We just hate that word don't we, especially those of us who think that we have sacrificed enough for our families. Well, just think about when we get to heaven and all the saints of old are sharing testimonies and boasting about what they went through for the sake of our Lord. Some literally went through fire, some were torn to bits, and others were sawn in pieces, hung and much worse. Our testimony would be ...*I never got 5 minutes to myself*... or better still, ...*my baby kept me awake at night!* My Dad showed me that if I needed a large block of time to complete a task, I would need to lose sleep for it. So, for 2 nights each week, after the kids were in bed, I would stay up, after drinking a nourishment drink, for about 5 or 6 hours and complete tasks. When I considered that my life vision might not be fulfilled if I did not do that or something similar, there was no question of its necessity. I made sure that I chose nights when I could have a late lie-in the next morning and didn't have anything too mentally strenuous to do the next day. I also prepared myself to be tired the next day, so I just decided not to be miserable and made sure that I ate well. Now, I am not giving you any new commandments here, but I am trying to throw you a lifeline; something to help you to get more done than change nappies a million times, vacuum the carpet 250 times and wash 3500 items of kitchenware!

The 'Made It' Wife

There is only one appropriate analogy that I can use to discuss the husband and wife and partnership. And that is of Christ and the Church. This depiction makes it easy for us to learn some valuable lessons about wifehood. If we are a type of the church and our hubbies are a type of Christ, then obviously we should behave towards our husbands, as the church should to our Lord. 'Easier said than done' I can hear you thinking. Yes, I know that he really knows how to bug you like no other man can, but this book was written more for you than him, so I'll stick to what you need to do. I will give you some advice that my Dad gave to me.

Shut up and pray! Let me put it into context for you. When something that he does bothers you; communicate. Tell him how you feel. Please try not to tell

SHUT UP AND PRAY!

him with raised voice or tears, but however you do it just tell him. Then if there seems to be no real acknowledgement, tell Daddy all about it. It's important that you speak to your husband, about the things that matter to you, it might help to speak to Dad first, but don't expect Him to tell him how you are feeling and what you are thinking. He won't, but one thing He will do is talk to you about how you, *yes you*, need to change. So after you explain to him that his socks won't walk into the laundry basket by themselves, (with more humour than sarcasm), leave it alone. If you find yourself kicking a slightly smelly pair of socks under the sofa, because you have spontaneous visitors, do not give him the look, and do not even mention it again. Pray. And watch Dad work it out. Believe it or not, sometimes you will be in the wrong, and Daddy will let you know, but you will find that however it works out, Daddy will see your good intentions and give you peace. The bottom line is, don't sweat it. You should come to the place where you enjoy your husband when he is good and when he is not so good. And in the not so good times, you will talk once and pray forever if necessary. But you will not allow any minor thing, (and it is the minor things that stink so much); get in the way of your joy, your peace and your relationship with your Dad. Now that the boring bit is out of the way, let's get on with the fun bit.

As well as being commanded to respect our husbands, we are also commanded to enjoy them. Now all you newlyweds can feel free to skip this bit if you want to or if you do want a bit of a reminder, here goes. Remember when you were single and desperately pining for someone to love you exclusively and to whom you could literally bare all and be accepted and wanted and cherished. Well, he's here and my advice to you in the area of bedroom ethics is unless there are exceptional circumstances or a time of fasting, don't say no! One of my elderly friends often said to me that when her  late husband would approach her for intercourse, she would use it as a sport to find different reasons why she couldn't. She was either tired, angry, scared of getting pregnant etc., but then he became very ill, and could no longer make sexual advances. She spent a lot of time advising me not to make her same mistake. She warned me not to set myself up to have regrets, as she did, about what she took for granted then, but craved for now. As she so eloquently put it, the older you get, the more you want it!!

One word that encapsulates the mindset of a 'made it' wife is commitment. There will be hard times as well as the great times and there may be the stage that some call the '7 year bump'. I am not a fantasy person, so I won't lie to you and make you believe that your marriage will be plain sailing. You are going to have to work hard at it. You will have to make sure that you do your best. Notice the emphasis on *you* and not him, because you cannot change him, you can only change yourself. But the irony is you can change him, by changing yourself. If you behave or speak in a different way, you will get a different response. Take charge of yourself; do not allow a weakling's mindset to take over you. You are strong, so use your strength to stay committed to him. When others turn against him, he should be confident that you will stay. When others talk about him, he should know that you will not. When he is lonely, sad, angry or frustrated, he should feel free to talk, because he knows that you will listen and love. And that even when you do not agree with what he has said or done, you will still agree with him, and that you will be there. By his side. Come what may. Committed.

Homework

TASK FIVE
- Do an audit of all your roles.
- In which roles do you shine?
- In which roles could you shine brighter?

Lesson 6

Stand Up! (Unless you're Rosa Parks)

Stand fast therefore in the liberty wherewith Christ hath made us free, and be not entangled again in the yoke of bondage.
(Galatians 5 v1)

The day that I am writing this Lesson is the day that a great woman passed from this life into eternity. At 92 years of age, Rosa Parks left this land after making a significant contribution to the lives and freedom of those she has left behind. By refusing to see herself as any less than any other person on that bus, she made the way for every other black person in America to be able to sit where they want to on any bus. Not just that, by her actions, she told every oppressed person who has heard her story that they do not have to just sit there and take it. There is always something that can be done to remove tyranny. No woman, (man or child for that matter), should have to live their lives under oppression. Christ sacrificed everything that He had, so that you could be free. So do not allow bullies into your life. It is important that you clearly know and understand your God-given life's purpose, so that you can dismiss anything or anyone who comes into your life to steer you off track. A woman of colour can be an issue for some people. Some people honestly have a problem with the colour of another person's skin. Miriam and Aaron in the Bible had a problem with the skin colour of Moses' wife, but God did not, after all He gave her that hue. A lot of the time, when skin colour is an issue for some people, ignorance is the real cause and if it is not ignorance, it is fear. Some people are actually afraid of your greatness. They are afraid of the wonders you will do, and what you will contribute to the world if you are free, so they try to keep you bound. It was the self-confession of Pharaoh when he saw the Israelites growing in number. He was afraid that they might grow so large that he wouldn't be able to control them, so he tried to control them through oppression. But guess what, that did not stop them from growing. If anything, they grew even more. There is nothing like real hardship to make you all snugly and united with your mate! When people around you try to keep you tied up, (or even tied to the kitchen sink), by using negative words, actions, non-verbal communication or anything else, recognise it for what it is, see the greatness inside of you and grow all the more. Yes, a lot of us choose to be the main housekeeper, and for some of us the art of keeping the house orderly is our ministry, however, for the majority of us, it is something that we do, it is not who we are. I am currently occupying the role of homemaker, but please do not misunderstand me, I not only take my role seriously, I see it as a valuable and blessed, (although tiring), position to be in. At the same time, God has been challenging me to do some of the other things that He has placed in my heart to do. Although I seem to have no time for myself, the Lord has shown me that I can write a portion of this book every day for 5 minutes a day and it will get done. And guess what, it got done. My husband was quite conventionally minded about marital roles when we first got married. However, the other day, out of the blue, he started praying for me and in his prayers he began to loose me into my destiny. These were his words, 'I release Monica now, from the pots and pans and I pray for helpers to come into her life.' I say all of this to say that I had to first value my freedom and purpose in life, before God enabled other people to see how important it was for me to be released from activities that could be delegated, so that I could be free to realise my potential. Allow no one to keep you from giving birth to your brainchild. It has never been more urgent for God's people to be obedient to Him. When He comes back for us, it will not be good enough for us to tell Him that 'my children wouldn't let me,' or ' my husband wouldn't let me,' or 'my boss wouldn't let me.' So. Unless your name is Rosa Parks, STAND UP!

Stand

To

Attention

Never

Deny

Ur

Potential

Homework

TASK SIX

If you're feeling poetic, write a poem with the theme FREEDOM.

Lesson 7
Daddy's Girls

You have received the Spirit of adoption, whereby we cry, Abba Father.
(Romans 8 v15)

The benchmark that I use for myself as a parent is the one that my Heavenly Father has set. When I want to know if I am being too harsh with Jerry, I ask for my Dad's opinion on the matter and He usually says 'to the merciful, I will show mercy.' More specifically, my husband uses God's example of Fatherhood to me, to guide him in being a father to Jahdai. Let us look at some examples:

Before Dad started increasing how much money He gave me, He first taught me how to manage money. He allowed me to experience doing without, so that I would appreciate it when it came. A father's tendency is to buy every and anything that their daughter wants. But think about the long-term effect of doing this. Your daughter will probably only accept a marriage proposal from a man who can afford to buy her anything that she wants and she may miss out on the excitement of contributing to the building of their life together. She may also rely too much on a man to provide for her, so that she feels that she cannot do things for herself. Teach your daughter to be financially astute; it will serve her well in the future.

Next, Dad did and still does provide for me. Although He taught me discipline, He provided food, clothing, shelter and much more for me, at the same time. So there was always much to give Him thanks for. Dads have a God-given responsibility to provide for their children. I struggled with this one for a while. Because my biological dad wasn't around to give me regular pocket money etc, I found it hard to accept things from people and from God. I wasn't confident enough to allow others to see that I had a need. But thank God, I'm over that now, I know the exact shade, size and price of the dress that what I want for my birthday this year!!

Dads are supposed to compliment their daughters, (as well as their wives and sons). A pastor friend always calls his daughter 'gorgeous', and quite rightly so. It is important for our daughters to grow up hearing that they are pretty, clever and resourceful. When they are older, they will easily gravitate to people who speak positive words into their lives.

The most valuable thing that my Heavenly Dad has given to me is a promise; that He will never leave me nor forsake me. If there is one thing that every little girl needs to know is that daddy is there for her. If anyone tries to bully her, daddy will sort it out. If a guy breaks her heart, daddy will make it better. I know that fathering daughters is a tall order, but I also know that you can do it, if you look to the One who Fathered me, and remember that He is the Father of all creation.

Homework

TASK SEVEN
Read these quotes from real-life dads on advice for bringing up daughters:

> "Be your daughter's hero."
> *Paul Grey*

> "How I treat my wife strongly indicates to my daughter how I expect her to be treated by her husband."
> *Ian Brown*

> "Pay attention to your daughter, or else later on you'll be competing with other men."
> *Alex Gordon*

> "Be prepared to spend an enormous amount of time paying attention to your daughter."
> *Isaac Carter*

> "My daughters are 'challenge', 'joy' and 'deepest love'. They make me say daily, *'thank You for these girls Lord'*."
> *Garrett Brooks*

> "Be there for her."
> *Richard Ansah*

"Love note Gen. 1:27
My daughter,

Did you catch that? You are made in my image. You are worthy, not for what you do, how you look or what you own ... but because I made you.

-Your loving Father."

(NIV, Zondervan, true images, The Bible for teen girls).

Please feel free to contact us
by emailing
info@daddysgirls.co.uk

ALSO PUBLISHED BY GREY SERVICES

Change Starts From Within
Written by Paul Grey
Illustrated by Natasha Williams

Paul Grey's autobiographical account of his journey through the Mental Health system.

"Your book is simply brilliant and apt. I use [it] now as an aide-memoir for my journey called 'life'... The community needs your book."

"Change Starts From Within...provided me with a great snap shot into your life in the mental health institute and how you manage[d] to turn your life around. I am going to read it with my sons because for me there are important messages about life within your book for [my] partner, my children & me."

Buy it now from Amazon.co.uk or www.changestartsfromwithin.co.uk